Easy Pizza Cookbook

50 Delicious Pizza Recipes

By
BookSumo Press
All rights reserved

Published by
http://www.booksumo.com

ENJOY THE RECIPES?

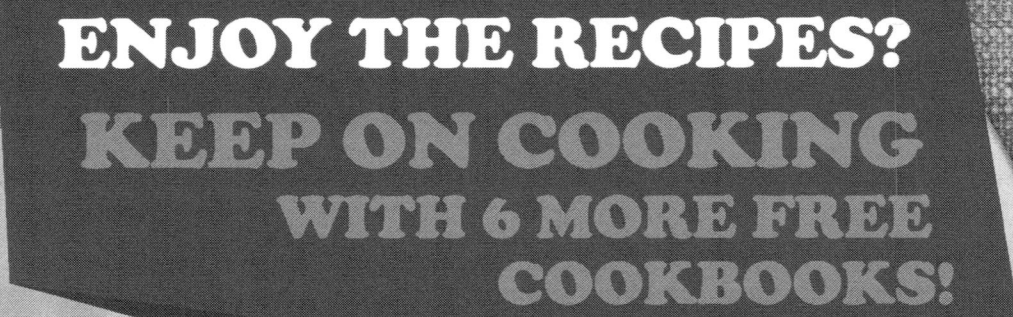

KEEP ON COOKING WITH 6 MORE FREE COOKBOOKS!

Visit our website and simply enter your email address to join the club and receive your 6 cookbooks.

http://booksumo.com/magnet

https://www.instagram.com/booksumopress/

https://www.facebook.com/booksumo/

LEGAL NOTES

All Rights Reserved. No Part Of This Book May Be Reproduced Or Transmitted In Any Form Or By Any Means. Photocopying, Posting Online, And / Or Digital Copying Is Strictly Prohibited Unless Written Permission Is Granted By The Book's Publishing Company. Limited Use Of The Book's Text Is Permitted For Use In Reviews Written For The Public.

Table of Contents

Cold Vegetable Pizza 7

How To Make Pizza Dough 8

Lunchbox Pizza 9

Chilled Fruity Treat 10

Smoky Pizza 11

Sweet-Tooth Pizza 12

Artisan Pizza 13

Unique Pizza 14

Pepperoni Pizza Dip 15

Tuna Pizza 16

Delish Pizza Flavored Chicken 17

Breakfast Pizza 18

Garden Fresh Pizza 19

Pizza Shells 20

Hot Italian Skillet Pizza 21

New Orleans Style Pizza 22

Thursday Night Pizza 23

Hamburger Pizza 25

Mixed Veggie Pizza 26

Cream of Pizza 27

Roma Fontina Pizza 28

Spicy Spinach Chicken Pizza 29

Super-Bowl Pizza 31

Applewood Flatbread Pizza 33

Early Morning Pizza 34

Pennsylvanian Style Pizza 35

Backroad Pizza 36

Buttermilk Pizza 37

Kid's Friendly Pizzas 38

Worcestershire Pizza 39

BBQ Beef Pizza 40

Mexican Style Pizza 41

Mediterranean Pizza 43

Pizza Rigatoni 44

All Peppers and Onions Pizza 45

I ♥ Pizza 46

Vegetarian Potato Tofu Pizza 47

Greek Pizza 49

Pizza Salad 50

Little Tike Dessert Pizza 52

Picnic Mini Pizzas 53

Tropical Walnut Pizza 54

Cranberry Chicken Pizza 55

Sweet & Salty Pizza 56

Autumnal Dijon Pizza 58

Mediterranean Pizza II 59

Gorgonzola Buttery Pizza 60

Arugula Grape Pizza 61

French Style Pizza 62

Cold Vegetable Pizza

Prep Time: 25 mins
Total Time: 2 hrs 50 mins

Servings per Recipe: 16
Calories   196 kcal
Fat   12.6 g
Carbohydrates   16 g
Protein   4.8 g
Cholesterol   36 mg
Sodium   359 mg

Ingredients

- 2 (8 oz.) packages refrigerated crescent rolls
- 1 C. sour cream
- 1 (8 oz.) package cream cheese, softened
- 1 tsp dried dill weed
- 1/4 tsp garlic salt
- 1 (1 oz.) package ranch dressing mix
- 1 small onion, finely chopped
- 1 stalk celery, thinly sliced
- 1/2 C. halved and thinly-sliced radishes
- 1 red bell pepper, chopped
- 1 1/2 C. fresh broccoli, chopped
- 1 carrot, grated

Directions

1. Set your oven to 350 degrees F before doing anything else and grease a jellyroll pan.
2. Place the crescent roll dough into the prepared jellyroll pan and keep everything aside for about 25 minutes.
3. With a fork, pierce the dough, roll it and cook everything in the oven for about 10 minutes.
4. Remove everything from the oven and keep it aside to cool for about 10 minutes.
5. In a bowl, mix together the cream cheese, sour cream, garlic, dill weed, ranch dip and salt.
6. Place the cream cheese mixture over the crust evenly.
7. Arrange the vegetables over the cream cheese mixture evenly.
8. Refrigerate to chill, covered.
9. Cut the dish into desired slices and serve.

HOW TO MAKE
Pizza Dough

Prep Time: 10 mins
Total Time: 2 hrs 34 mins

Servings per Recipe: 6
Calories	262 kcal
Fat	4.4 g
Carbohydrates	46g
Protein	6.2 g
Cholesterol	10 mg
Sodium	418 mg

Ingredients

1 C. water
2 tbsp butter
2 tbsp sugar
1 tsp salt

2 1/2 C. all-purpose flour
2 1/4 tsp yeast

Directions

1. In a bread machine, add the water, butter, sugar, salt, flour, and yeast in the order recommended by the manufacturer.
2. Select the Dough setting, and press Start.
3. After cycle is complete, remove the dough from the bread machine.
4. In a greased pizza pan, place the dough by pressing it, then brush with the oil.
5. Keep aside, covered for about 15 minutes.
6. Set your oven to 400 degrees F.
7. Spread the sauce and topping of your choice and cook everything in the oven for about 24 minutes.

Lunchbox Pizza

Prep Time: 5 mins
Total Time: 20 mins

Servings per Recipe: 1
Calories	405 kcal
Fat	18 g
Carbohydrates	39.9g
Protein	19.7 g
Cholesterol	44 mg
Sodium	1156 mg

Ingredients

- 1 pita bread round
- 1 tsp olive oil
- 3 tbsp pizza sauce
- 1/2 C. shredded mozzarella cheese
- 1/4 C. sliced crimini mushrooms
- 1/8 tsp garlic salt

Directions

1. Set your grill for medium-high heat and grease the grill grate.
2. Spread the oil and pizza sauce over 1 side of the pita bread evenly.
3. Place the mushrooms and cheese over the sauce and sprinkle everything with the garlic salt.
4. Arrange the pita bread onto the grill, mushrooms side up.
5. Cover and cook on the grill for about 5 minutes.

CHILLED
Fruity Treat

Prep Time: 10 mins
Total Time: 20 mins

Servings per Recipe: 16
Calories	235 kcal
Fat	12.8 g
Carbohydrates	28g
Protein	2.3 g
Cholesterol	19 mg
Sodium	164 mg

Ingredients

1 (18 oz.) package refrigerated sugar cookie dough
1 (7 oz.) jar marshmallow creme
1 (8 oz.) package cream cheese, softened

Directions

1. Set your oven to 350 degrees F before doing anything else.
2. Place the dough on a medium baking sheet about 1/4-inch thick.
3. Cook everything in the oven for about 10 minutes.
4. Remove everything from the oven and keep it aside to cool.
5. In a bowl, mix together the cream cheese and marshmallow crème.
6. Spread the cream cheese mixture over the crust and refrigerate to chill before serving.

Smoky Pizza

Prep Time: 20 mins
Total Time: 20 mins

Servings per Recipe: 8
Calories	310 kcal
Fat	10.8 g
Carbohydrates	45.6 g
Protein	6.9 g
Cholesterol	2 mg
Sodium	542 mg

Ingredients

- 3 1/2 C. all-purpose flour
- 1 envelope Fleischmann's(R) Pizza Crust Yeast
- 1 tbsp sugar
- 1 1/2 tsp salt
- 1 1/3 C. very warm water (120 degrees to 130 degrees F)
- 1/3 C. oil
- Additional flour for rolling
- Additional oil for grilling
- Pizza sauce
- Other toppings as desired
- Shredded mozzarella cheese

Directions

1. Set your grill for medium-high heat and grease the grill grate.
2. In a large bowl, mix together 2 C. of the flour, yeast, sugar and salt.
3. Add the oil and water and mix till well combined.
4. Slowly, add the remaining flour and mix till a slightly sticky dough forms.
5. Place the dough on a floured surface and knead it till the dough becomes elastic.
6. Divide the dough into 8 portions and roll each portion on a floured surface into about 8-inch circle.
7. Coat both sides of each crust with some extra oil.
8. Cook all the crusts on the grill for about 3-4 minutes.
9. Transfer the crust onto a smooth surface, grilled side up.
10. Spread a thin layer of pizza sauce onto each crust evenly.
11. Place your desired toppings and cheese over the sauce and cook everything on the grill till the cheese melts.

SWEET-TOOTH
Pizza

Prep Time: 15 mins
Total Time: 30 mins

Servings per Recipe: 12
Calories   261 kcal
Fat   13.5 g
Carbohydrates   33.9 g
Protein   2.2 g
Cholesterol   12 mg
Sodium   182 mg

Ingredients

1 (18 oz.) package refrigerated sugar cookie dough
1 (8 oz.) container frozen whipped topping, thawed
1/2 C. sliced banana
1/2 C. sliced fresh strawberries
1/2 C. crushed pineapple, drained
1/2 C. seedless grapes, halved

Directions

1. Set your oven to 350 degrees F before doing anything else.
2. Place the dough on a 12-inch pizza pan.
3. Cook everything in the oven for about 15-20 minutes.
4. Remove everything from the oven and keep it aside to cool.
5. Spread the whipped topping over the crust and top with the fruit in any desired design.
6. Refrigerate to chill before serving.

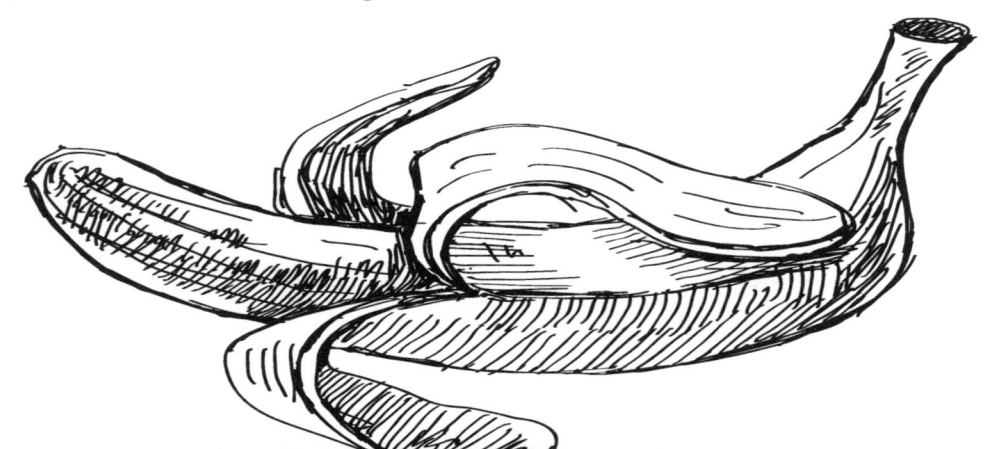

Artisan Pizza

Prep Time: 10 mins
Total Time: 20 mins

Servings per Recipe: 6
Calories	394 kcal
Fat	19.9 g
Carbohydrates	39.3g
Protein	17.3 g
Cholesterol	36 mg
Sodium	937 mg

Ingredients

- 1 (12 inch) pre-baked pizza crust
- 1/2 C. pesto
- 1 ripe tomato, chopped
- 1/2 C. green bell pepper, chopped
- 1 (2 oz.) can chopped black olives, drained
- 1/2 small red onion, chopped
- 1 (4 oz.) can artichoke hearts, drained and sliced
- 1 C. crumbled feta cheese

Directions

1. Set your oven to 450 degrees F before doing anything else.
2. Place the dough on a pizza pan.
3. Place a thin layer of the pesto over the crust evenly and top with the vegetables and feta cheese.
4. Sprinkle the pizza with the cheese and cook everything in the oven for about 8-10 minutes.

UNIQUE
Pizza

🥣 Prep Time: 15 mins
🕐 Total Time: 30 mins

Servings per Recipe: 8
Calories	251 kcal
Fat	12.5 g
Carbohydrates	22.3g
Protein	12.7 g
Cholesterol	25 mg
Sodium	495 mg

Ingredients

- 1 (10 oz.) can refrigerated pizza crust dough
- 1 C. hummus spread
- 1 1/2 C. sliced bell peppers, any color
- 1 C. broccoli florets
- 2 C. shredded Monterey Jack cheese

Directions

1. Set your oven to 475 degrees F before doing anything else.
2. Place the dough on a pizza pan.
3. Place a thin layer of the hummus over the crust evenly and top everything with the broccoli and bell peppers.
4. Sprinkle the pizza with the cheese and cook everything in the oven for about 10-15 minutes.

Pepperoni Pizza Dip

Prep Time: 10 mins
Total Time: 35 mins

Servings per Recipe: 8
Calories   305 kcal
Fat   24.5 g
Carbohydrates   8.6 g
Protein   12.6 g
Cholesterol   68 mg
Sodium   944 mg

Ingredients

- 1 (8 oz.) package cream cheese, softened
- 1 (14 oz.) can pizza sauce
- 1/4 lb. pepperoni sausage, diced
- 1 onion, chopped
- 1 (6 oz.) can black olives, chopped
- 2 C. shredded mozzarella cheese

Directions

1. Set your oven to 400 degrees F before doing anything else and grease a 9-inch pie pan.
2. In the bottom of the prepared of pie pan, place the cream cheese and top with the pizza sauce.
3. Top everything with the olives, pepperoni and onion and sprinkle with mozzarella cheese.
4. Cook everything in the oven for about 20-25 minutes.

TUNA
Pizza

🥣 Prep Time: 10 mins
🕐 Total Time: 30 mins

Servings per Recipe: 8
Calories   323 kcal
Fat   16.3 g
Carbohydrates   27g
Protein   18.4 g
Cholesterol   54 mg
Sodium   512 mg

Ingredients

1 (8 oz.) package cream cheese, softened
1 (14 oz.) package pre-baked pizza crust
1 (5 oz.) can tuna, drained and flaked
1/2 C. thinly sliced red onion

1 1/2 C. shredded mozzarella cheese
crushed red pepper flakes, or to taste

Directions

1. Set your oven to 400 degrees F before doing anything else.
2. Spread the cream cheese over the pre-baked crust.
3. Top the crust with the tuna and onions and sprinkle with the mozzarella cheese and red pepper flakes.
4. Cook everything in the oven for about 15-20 minutes.

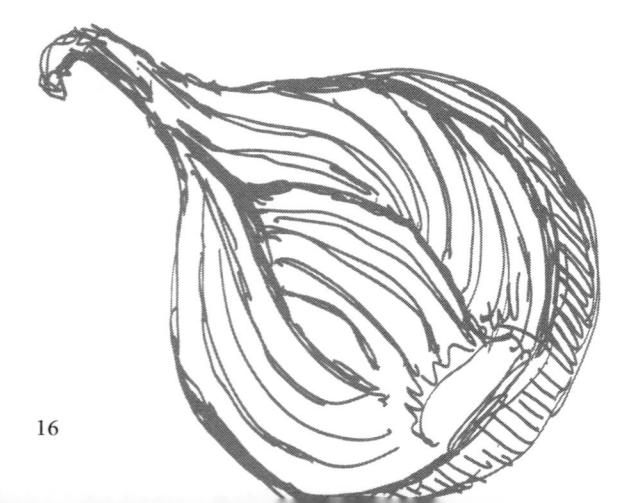

Delish
Pizza Flavored Chicken

Prep Time: 15 mins
Total Time: 45 mins

Servings per Recipe: 2
Calories   552 kcal
Fat   16 g
Carbohydrates   52.9g
Protein   46.2 g
Cholesterol   185 mg
Sodium   2497 mg

Ingredients

- 1/2 C. Italian-seasoned bread crumbs
- 1/4 C. grated Parmesan cheese
- 1 tsp salt
- 1 tsp ground black pepper
- 1/2 C. all-purpose flour
- 1 egg
- 1 tbsp lemon juice
- 2 skinless, boneless chicken breast halves
- 1/2 C. pizza sauce, divided
- 1/2 C. shredded mozzarella cheese, divided
- 4 slices pepperoni, or to taste - divided

Directions

1. Set your oven to 400 degrees F before doing anything else.
2. In a shallow dish, add the lemon juice and egg and beat well.
3. In a second shallow bowl, place the flour.
4. In a third bowl, mix together the Parmesan, bread crumbs, salt and black pepper.
5. Coat each chicken breast with the egg mixture and roll into the flour mixture.
6. Again dip the chicken in the egg mixture and roll into the breadcrumbs mixture.
7. Arrange the chicken breasts into a baking dish and cook everything in the oven for about 20 minutes.
8. Place about 2 tbsp of the pizza sauce over each chicken breast and top with the cheese and pepperoni slices evenly.
9. Cook everything in the oven for about 10 minutes.

BREAKFAST
Pizza

🥣 Prep Time: 20 mins
🕐 Total Time: 45 mins

Servings per Recipe: 10
Calories   201 kcal
Fat   8.5 g
Carbohydrates   20 g
Protein   10.3 g
Cholesterol   97 mg
Sodium   614 mg

Ingredients

- 2/3 C. warm water
- 1 (.25 oz.) package instant yeast
- 1/2 tsp salt
- 1 tsp white sugar
- 1/4 tsp dried oregano
- 1 3/4 C. all-purpose flour
- 6 slices turkey bacon, chopped
- 1/2 C. green onion, thinly sliced
- 6 eggs, beaten
- salt and pepper to taste
- 1/2 C. pizza sauce
- 1/4 C. grated Parmesan cheese
- 2 oz. thinly sliced salami

Directions

1. Set your oven to 400 degrees F before doing anything else and lightly grease a pizza tray.
2. In a bowl, add the water, sugar, yeast, oregano and salt and stir till dissolved completely.
3. Add about 1 C. of the flour and mix well.
4. Add the remaining flour and mix well.
5. With a plastic wrap, cover the bowl and keep aside for about 10-15 minutes.
6. Heat a large skillet on medium heat and cook the bacon till browned completely.
7. Add the green onions and stir fry for about 1 minute.
8. Add the eggs and cook, stirring till the scrambled eggs are prepared.
9. Stir in the salt and black pepper.
10. Spread the pizza sauce over the dough and place the dough onto the prepared pizza tray.
11. Top with the bacon, eggs, Parmesan and salami and cook everything in the oven for about 20-25 minutes.

Garden Fresh Pizza

Prep Time: 45 mins
Total Time: 9 hrs 25 mins

Servings per Recipe: 30
Calories   138 kcal
Fat   10.5 g
Carbohydrates   8.2 g
Protein   2.6 g
Cholesterol   18 mg
Sodium   233 mg

Ingredients

- 2 (8 oz.) packages refrigerated crescent rolls
- 2 (8 oz.) packages cream cheese, softened
- 1/3 C. mayonnaise
- 1 (1.4 oz.) package dry vegetable soup mix
- 1 C. radishes, sliced
- 1/3 C. chopped green bell pepper
- 1/3 C. chopped red bell pepper
- 1/3 C. chopped yellow bell pepper
- 1 C. broccoli florets
- 1 C. cauliflower florets
- 1/2 C. chopped carrot
- 1/2 C. chopped celery

Directions

1. Set your oven to 400 degrees F before doing anything else.
2. In the bottom of an 11x14-inch jellyroll pan, spread the crescent roll dough.
3. With your fingers, pinch any seams together to make a crust.
4. Cook everything in the oven for about 10 minutes.
5. Remove everything from the oven and keep it aside to cool completely.
6. In a bowl, mix together the mayonnaise, cream cheese and vegetable soup mix.
7. Place the mayonnaise mixture over the crust evenly and top everything with the vegetables evenly and gently press them into mayonnaise mixture.
8. With the plastic wrap, cover the pizza and refrigerate it overnight.

PIZZA
Shells

Prep Time: 30 mins
Total Time: 1 hr 30 mins

Servings per Recipe: 6
Calories	637 kcal
Fat	30.4 g
Carbohydrates	66.5g
Protein	28.3 g
Cholesterol	63 mg
Sodium	1139 mg

Ingredients

2 (28 oz.) cans crushed tomatoes
2 tbsp canola oil
2 tbsp dried oregano
1 tsp dried basil
1 tsp white sugar
1 (12 oz.) box jumbo pasta shells
1 (6 oz.) can sliced mushrooms, drained
1/2 green bell pepper, chopped
1/2 onion, chopped
2 C. shredded Monterey Jack cheese
1 (6 oz.) package of sliced mini pepperoni

Directions

1. In a pan, add the crushed tomatoes, basil, oregano, sugar and oil and mix well.
2. Cover the pan and bring to a boil.
3. Reduce the heat to low and simmer for about 30 minutes.
4. Set your oven to 350 degrees F.
5. In a large pan of lightly salted boiling water, cook the pasta shells for about 10 minutes, stirring occasionally.
6. Drain well and keep aside.
7. In a bowl, mix together the green pepper, onion and mushroom.
8. Place about 1 tsp of the tomato sauce in each shell and sprinkle with the onion mixture and about 1 tbsp of the Monterey Jack cheese.
9. In a 13x9-inch baking dish, arrange the shells, side by side and touching and place mini pepperoni slices over each shell.
10. Cook everything in the oven for about 30 minutes.

Hot Italian Skillet Pizza

Prep Time: 15 mins
Total Time: 40 mins

Servings per Recipe: 2
Calories	323 kcal
Fat	25.2 g
Carbohydrates	13.2g
Protein	11.7 g
Cholesterol	46 mg
Sodium	554 mg

Ingredients

- 1 tbsp olive oil
- 1 Spanish onion, thinly sliced
- 1 green bell pepper, thinly sliced
- 1 (3.5 oz.) link hot Italian sausage, sliced
- 1/4 C. sliced fresh mushrooms, or more to taste
- 1 slice prepared polenta, cut into 4x4-inch piece
- 1/4 C. spaghetti sauce, or as needed
- 1 oz. shredded mozzarella cheese

Directions

1. In a large skillet, heat the oil on medium heat and sauté the sausage, bell pepper, mushrooms and onion for about 10-15 minutes.
2. Transfer the mixture into a large bowl.
3. In the same skillet, add the polenta and cook for about 5 minutes on both sides.
4. Top the polenta with the sausage mixture, followed by the spaghetti sauce and mozzarella cheese.
5. Cook for about 5-10 minutes.

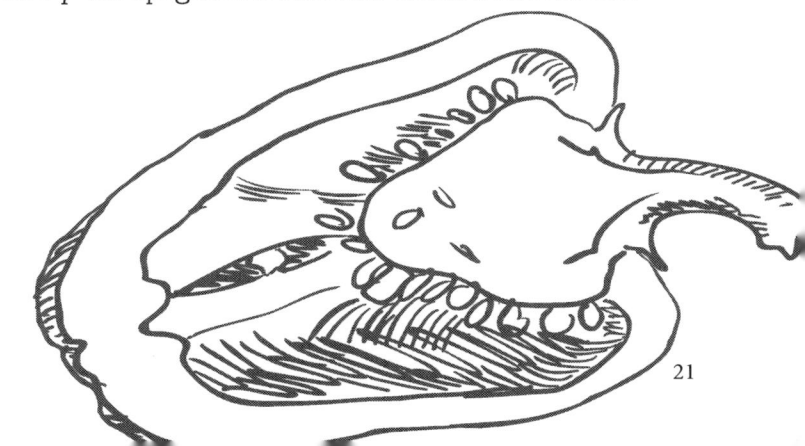

NEW ORLEANS
Style Pizza

🥣 Prep Time: 45 mins
🕐 Total Time: 1 hr

Servings per Recipe: 6
Calories   511 kcal
Fat   29.1 g
Carbohydrates   38.4g
Protein   22.5 g
Cholesterol   52 mg
Sodium   1631 mg

Ingredients

8 jumbo black olives, pitted
8 pitted green olives
2 tbsp chopped celery
2 tbsp chopped red onion
2 cloves chopped garlic
6 leaves chopped fresh basil
1 tbsp chopped fresh parsley
2 tbsp olive oil
1/2 tsp dried oregano
salt and freshly ground black pepper to taste
1 (16 oz.) package ready-made pizza crust
1 tbsp olive oil
1/2 tsp garlic powder to taste
salt to taste
2 oz. shredded mozzarella cheese
2 oz. shredded provolone cheese
2 oz. grated Parmesan cheese
2 oz. thinly sliced hard salami, cut into strips
2 oz. thinly sliced mortadella, cut into strips
4 oz. thinly sliced prosciutto, cut into strips

Directions

1. In a bowl, mix together the olives, onion, celery, garlic, fresh herbs, dried oregano, salt, black pepper and oil.
2. Cover and refrigerate to chill before using.
3. Set your oven to 500 degrees F.
4. Brush the pizza crust with the oil and sprinkle with the garlic powder and salt.
5. Arrange the pizza crust over the oven rack and cook everything in the oven for about 5 minutes.
6. Remove everything from the oven and keep it aside to cool completely.
7. Now, set the oven to broiler.
8. In a bowl, mix together all the remaining ingredients.
9. Add the olive mixture and stir to combine.
10. Place the mixture over the crust evenly and cook under the broiler for about 5 minutes.
11. Cut the dish into the desired slices and serve.

Thursday Night Pizza

Prep Time: 2 hrs
Total Time: 2 hrs 20 mins

Servings per Recipe: 16
Calories	338 kcal
Fat	16.1 g
Carbohydrates	32.7g
Protein	14.8 g
Cholesterol	42 mg
Sodium	708 mg

Ingredients

- 10 fluid oz. warm water
- 3/4 tsp salt
- 3 tbsp vegetable oil
- 4 C. all-purpose flour
- 2 tsp active dry yeast
- 1 (6 oz.) can tomato paste
- 3/4 C. water
- 1 (1.25 oz.) package taco seasoning mix, divided
- 1 tsp chili powder
- 1/2 tsp cayenne pepper
- 1 (16 oz.) can fat-free refried beans
- 1/3 C. salsa
- 1/4 C. chopped onion
- 1/2 lb. ground beef
- 4 C. shredded Cheddar cheese

Directions

1. In the bread machine, add the water, salt, oil, flour and yeast in the order recommended by the manufacturer.
2. Select the dough cycle.
3. Check the dough after a few minutes.
4. If it is too dry and not mixing slowly, add water 1 tbsp at a time, until it is mixing and has a nice pliable dough consistency.
5. Meanwhile, in a small bowl, mix together the tomato paste, 3/4 of the package of taco seasoning mix, cayenne pepper, chili powder and water.
6. In another bowl, mix together the salsa, refried beans and onion.
7. Heat a large skillet and cook the ground beef till browned completely.

8. Drain the excess grease from the skillet.
9. Add the remaining 1/4 package of taco seasoning and a small amount of water and simmer for a few minutes.
10. Remove everything from the heat.
11. Set your oven to 400 degrees F before continuing.
12. After the dough cycle is finished, remove the dough from the machine.
13. Divide the dough into 2 portions and place into two 12-inch pans.
14. Spread a layer of the bean mixture over each dough, followed by a layer of the tomato paste mixture, beef mixture and cheddar cheese.
15. Cook everything in the oven for about 10-15 minutes, turning halfway through the baking time.

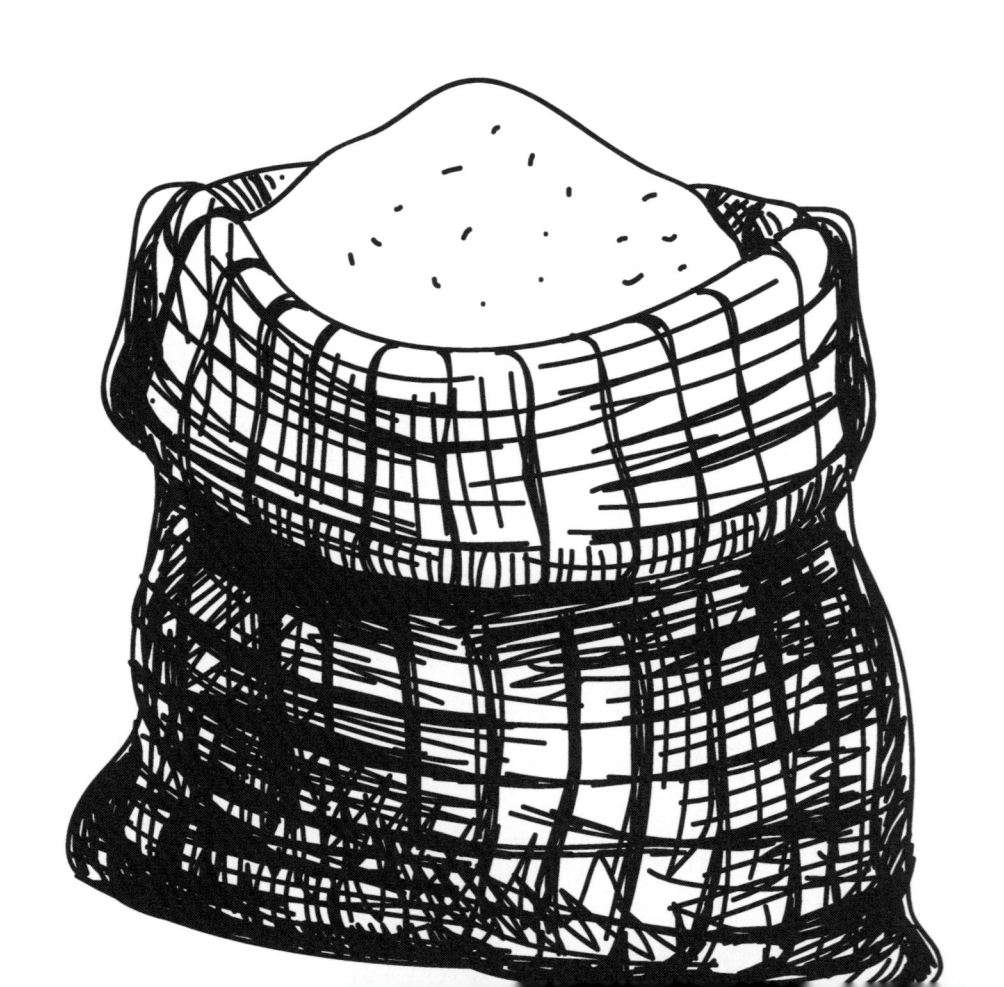

Hamburger Pizza

Prep Time: 10 mins
Total Time: 45 mins

Servings per Recipe: 8
Calories	341 kcal
Fat	14.4 g
Carbohydrates	29 g
Protein	22.3 g
Cholesterol	55 mg
Sodium	787 mg

Ingredients

- 8 hamburger buns, split
- 1 lb. ground beef
- 1/3 C. onion, chopped
- 1 (15 oz.) can pizza sauce
- 1/3 C. grated Parmesan cheese
- 2 1/4 tsp Italian seasoning
- 1 tsp garlic powder
- 1/4 tsp onion powder
- 1/8 tsp crushed red pepper flakes
- 1 tsp paprika
- 2 C. shredded mozzarella cheese

Directions

1. Set the oven to broiler and arrange the oven rack about 6-inches from the heating element.
2. In a baking sheet, arrange the bun halves, crust side down and cook everything under the broiler for about 1 minute.
3. Now, set the oven to 350 degrees F.
4. Heat a large skillet on medium heat and cook the beef for about 10 minutes.
5. Drain the excess grease from the skillet.
6. Stir in the onion and stir fry everything for about 5 minutes.
7. Add the remaining ingredients except the mozzarella cheese and bring to a boil.
8. Simmer, stirring occasionally for 10-15 minutes.
9. Arrange the buns on a baking sheet and top them with the beef mixture and mozzarella cheese evenly.
10. Cook everything in the oven for about 10 minutes.

MIXED VEGGIE Pizza

Prep Time: 10 mins
Total Time: 30 mins

Servings per Recipe: 4
Calories 417 kcal
Fat 17.4 g
Carbohydrates 45.5g
Protein 19.4 g
Cholesterol 33 mg
Sodium 1146 mg

Ingredients

- 1 tbsp olive oil
- 1 (12 oz.) bag mixed vegetables
- 1 (10 oz.) pre-baked whole wheat pizza crust
- 1 C. prepared pizza sauce
- 1 oz. sliced pepperoni
- 1 C. shredded mozzarella cheese

Directions

1. Set your oven to 450 degrees F before doing anything else.
2. In a large nonstick skillet, heat the oil on medium-high heat and cook the mixed veggies for about 10 minutes, stirring occasionally.
3. Place the pizza crust on a baking sheet.
4. Spread the pizza sauce over the crust evenly and top with the vegetable mixture, pepperoni and mozzarella cheese.
5. Cook everything in the oven for about 10 minutes

Cream of Pizza

Prep Time: 15 mins
Total Time: 45 mins

Servings per Recipe: 12
Calories	628 kcal
Fat	38.2 g
Carbohydrates	38.7g
Protein	34.1 g
Cholesterol	266 mg
Sodium	1424 mg

Ingredients

- 1 lb. ground sausage
- 2 (12 inch) prepared pizza crusts
- 12 eggs
- 3/4 C. milk
- salt and pepper to taste
- 1 (10.75 oz.) can condensed cream of celery soup
- 1 (3 oz.) can turkey bacon bits
- 1 small onion, minced
- 1 small green bell pepper, chopped
- 4 C. shredded Cheddar cheese

Directions

1. Set your oven to 400 degrees F before doing anything else.
2. Heat a large skillet on medium-high heat and cook the sausage till browned completely. Transfer the sausage on a paper towel lined plate to drain then crumble it. Meanwhile in a bowl, add the milk, eggs, salt and black pepper and beat well.
3. In the same skillet of sausage, scramble the eggs till set completely.
4. Arrange the pizza crusts upside down on the cookie sheets and cook everything in the oven for about 5-7 minutes. Remove the crusts from the oven and turn the opposite side up.
5. Spread about 1/2 can of the cream of celery soup on top of each crust.
6. Place 1/2 of egg mixture on each crust.
7. Place the bacon bits on 1 pizza and top the other pizza with the crumbled sausage.
8. Top each pizza with the onions, peppers and 2 C. of the cheese.
9. Cook everything in the oven, for about 25-30 minutes.

ROMA
Fontina Pizza

Prep Time: 15 mins
Total Time: 40 mins

Servings per Recipe: 8
Calories   551 kcal
Fat   25.6 g
Carbohydrates   54.4g
Protein   28.9 g
Cholesterol   58 mg
Sodium   1183 mg

Ingredients

- 1/4 C. olive oil
- 1 tbsp minced garlic
- 1/2 tsp sea salt
- 8 Roma tomatoes, sliced
- 2 (12 inch) pre-baked pizza crusts
- 8 oz. shredded Mozzarella cheese
- 4 oz. shredded Fontina cheese
- 10 fresh basil leaves, shredded
- 1/2 C. freshly grated Parmesan cheese
- 1/2 C. crumbled feta cheese

Directions

1. Set your oven to 400 degrees F before doing anything else.
2. In a bowl, mix together the tomatoes, garlic, oil and salt and keep it aside for about 15 minutes.
3. Coat each pizza crust with some of the tomato marinade.
4. Top everything with the Mozzarella and Fontina cheeses, followed by the tomatoes, basil, Parmesan and feta cheese.
5. Cook everything in the oven for about 10 minutes.

Spicy Spinach Chicken Pizza

Prep Time: 1 hr
Total Time: 2 hrs 15 mins

Servings per Recipe: 8
Calories   635 kcal
Fat   41.7 g
Carbohydrates   40.9 g
Protein   24.1 g
Cholesterol   181 mg
Sodium   879 mg

Ingredients

- 1 C. warm water
- 1 tbsp white sugar
- 1 (.25 oz.) package active dry yeast
- 2 tbsp vegetable oil
- 3 C. all-purpose flour
- 1 tsp salt
- 6 slices turkey bacon
- 6 tbsp butter
- 2 cloves garlic, minced
- 1 1/2 C. heavy cream
- 2 egg yolks
- 1/2 C. freshly grated Parmesan cheese
- 1/2 C. freshly grated Romano cheese
- 1/8 tsp ground nutmeg
- 1/2 tsp paprika
- 1/4 tsp cayenne pepper
- 1/4 tsp ground cumin
- 1/4 tsp crumbled dried thyme
- 1/8 tsp salt
- 1/8 tsp ground white pepper
- 1/8 tsp onion powder
- 2 skinless, boneless chicken breast halves
- 1 tbsp vegetable oil
- 1 C. shredded mozzarella cheese
- 1/2 C. baby spinach leaves
- 3 tbsp freshly grated Parmesan cheese
- 1 roma tomato, diced

Directions

1. In the work bowl of a large stand mixer, fitted with a dough hook, add the water, sugar, yeast, and 2 tbsp of the vegetable oil and mix for several seconds on low speed.
2. Stop the mixer and add the flour and salt and again start the mixer on low speed and mix until the flour mixture is combined with the yeast mixture completely.
3. Now, turn the speed to medium-low and machine-knead the dough for about 10 to 12 minutes.

4. Sprinkle the dough with the flour occasionally if it sticks to the sides of the bowl.
5. Shape the dough into a ball and place everything into a greased bowl and turn the dough in the bowl several times to coat with the oil evenly.
6. With a towel, cover the dough and keep it in a warm place for at least 30 minutes to 1 hour.
7. Heat a large skillet on medium-high heat and cook the bacon till browned completely.
8. Transfer the bacon on a paper towel lined plate to drain then chop it.
9. In a large skillet, melt the butter and on medium heat and sauté the garlic for about 1 minute.
10. Stir in the cream and egg yolks and beat till smooth.
11. Stir in about 1/2 C. of the Parmesan cheese, Romano cheese, nutmeg and salt and bring to a gentle simmer on low heat.
12. Simmer, stirring continuously for about 3-5 minutes.
13. Remove everything from the heat and keep aside.
14. Set your oven to 350 degrees F before continuing.
15. In a bowl, mix together the thyme, cumin, paprika, cayenne pepper, onion powder, 1/8 tsp of the salt and white pepper.
16. Rub one side of each chicken breast with the spice mixture evenly.
17. In a skillet, heat 1 tbsp of the vegetable oil on high heat and sear the chicken breasts, spiced side, for about 1 minute per side.
18. Transfer the chicken breasts on a baking sheet.
19. Cook everything in the oven for about 5-10 minutes, or until fully done.
20. Remove everything from the oven and cut into slices.
21. Place the pizza dough on a floured surface and punch it down, then and it roll out.
22. Place the pizza crust on a heavy baking sheet.
23. With a fork, poke several holes, in the crust and cook everything in the oven for about 5-7 minutes.
24. Remove everything from the oven and place the Alfredo sauce over the crust evenly, followed by the mozzarella cheese, chicken slices, spinach leaves, bacon and 3 tbsp of the Parmesan cheese.
25. Cook everything in the oven for about 15-20 minutes.
26. Serve with a topping of chopped Roma tomatoes.

Super-Bowl Pizza

Prep Time: 25 mins
Total Time: 1 hr 50 mins

Servings per Recipe: 8
Calories   440 kcal
Fat   28.2 g
Carbohydrates   32.5g
Protein   14.4 g
Cholesterol   43 mg
Sodium   627 mg

Ingredients

- 3 potatoes, scrubbed
- 6 slices turkey bacon
- 1 (6.5 oz.) package pizza crust mix
- 1/2 C. water
- 1/4 C. olive oil
- 1 tbsp butter, melted
- 1/4 tsp garlic powder
- 1/4 tsp dried Italian seasoning
- 1/2 C. sour cream
- 1/2 C. Ranch dressing
- 3 green onions, chopped
- 1 1/2 C. shredded mozzarella cheese
- 1/2 C. shredded Cheddar cheese

Directions

1. Set your oven to 450 degrees F before doing anything else.
2. With a fork, prick the potatoes several times and arrange them on a baking sheet.
3. Cook everything in the oven for about 50-60 minutes.
4. Remove everything from the oven and cool, then peel them.
5. Heat a large skillet on medium-high heat and cook the bacon for about 10 minutes.
6. Transfer the bacon on a paper towel lined plate to drain then crumble it.
7. Now, set the oven to 400 degrees F and lightly grease a pizza pan.
8. In a large bowl, add the pizza crust mix, oil and water and with a fork mix till well combined.
9. Place the dough on a lightly floured surface and knead for about 8 minutes.
10. Keep aside for about 5 minutes.
11. Shape the dough into a flat circle and arrange it in the prepared pizza pan, allowing the dough to

hang over the edge slightly.
12. Cook everything in the oven for about 5-6 minutes.
13. In a large bowl, mix together the potatoes, butter, garlic powder and Italian seasoning.
14. In a small bowl, mix together the sour cream and ranch dressing.
15. Place the sour cream mixture over the crust evenly and top with the potato mixture, followed by the bacon, onions, mozzarella cheese, and Cheddar cheese.
16. Cook everything in the oven for about 15-20 minutes.

Applewood Flatbread Pizza

Prep Time: 30 mins
Total Time: 1 hr 15 mins

Servings per Recipe: 6
Calories   332 kcal
Fat   16.2 g
Carbohydrates   33.6 g
Protein   16.4 g
Cholesterol   28 mg
Sodium   761 mg

Ingredients

- 1 tbsp olive oil
- 6 crimini mushrooms, sliced
- 3 cloves garlic, chopped
- 1 pinch salt and ground black pepper
- 1 tbsp olive oil
- 8 spears fresh asparagus, trimmed and cut into 2-inch pieces
- 1/2 lb. applewood-smoked turkey bacon, cut into 2-inch pieces
- 1 (12 inch) prepared flatbread pizza crust
- 3/4 C. prepared marinara sauce
- 1/2 C. shredded mozzarella cheese
- 1/2 C. shredded Asiago cheese

Directions

1. Set your oven to 400 degrees F before doing anything else and line a baking sheet with foil.
2. In a large skillet, heat 1 tbsp of the oil on medium heat and sauté the mushrooms, garlic, salt and black pepper for about 10 minutes. Remove everything from the heat and keep it aside.
3. In another large skillet, heat 1 tbsp of the oil on medium-high heat and cook the asparagus for about 8 minutes, stirring occasionally.
4. Transfer the asparagus into a bowl. Reduce heat to medium, and in the same skillet, cook the bacon for about 10 minutes. Transfer the bacon on a paper towel lined plate to drain.
5. Arrange the flatbread crust onto the prepared baking sheet.
6. Place the marinara sauce over the crust evenly, followed by the mushrooms mixture, asparagus, bacon, mozzarella cheese and Asiago cheese.
7. Cook everything in the oven for about 12-15 minutes.

EARLY MORNING
Pizza

🥣 Prep Time: 15 mins
🕒 Total Time: 8 hrs 55 mins

Servings per Recipe: 8
Calories   430 kcal
Fat   31.6 g
Carbohydrates   12.8g
Protein   22 g
Cholesterol   203 mg
Sodium   1106 mg

Ingredients

1 lb. ground beef sausage
1 (8 oz.) package refrigerated crescent roll dough, or as needed
8 oz. mild Cheddar cheese, shredded
6 eggs
1/2 C. milk
1/2 tsp salt
ground black pepper to taste

Directions

1. Set your oven to 425 degrees F before doing anything else.
2. Heat a large skillet on medium heat and cook the beef till browned completely.
3. Drain the excess grease from the skillet.
4. Place the crescent roll dough on a greased 13x9-inch baking dish.
5. Place the sausage and cheddar cheese over the crescent roll dough evenly.
6. With plastic wrap, cover the baking dish and refrigerate for about 8 hours to overnight.
7. Set your oven to 350 degrees F.
8. In a bowl, add the eggs, milk, salt, and black pepper and beat well.
9. Place the egg mixture over the sausage and cheese in the baking dish evenly.
10. With some foil, cover the baking dish and cook everything in the oven for about 20 minutes.
11. Now, set the oven to 325 degrees F before continuing.
12. Uncover the baking dish and cook everything in the oven for about 15-25 minutes.

Pennsylvanian Style Flatbread Pizza

Prep Time: 25 mins
Total Time: 1 hr

Servings per Recipe: 8
Calories   207 kcal
Fat   15.4 g
Carbohydrates   6.5g
Protein   11.6 g
Cholesterol   44 mg
Sodium   698 mg

Ingredients

1 (1 lb.) loaf frozen whole wheat bread dough, thawed
1/2 C. thousand island dressing
2 C. shredded Swiss cheese
6 oz. deli sliced corned beef, cut into strips
1 C. sauerkraut - rinsed and drained
1/2 tsp caraway seed
1/4 C. chopped dill pickles (optional)

Directions

1. Set your oven to 375 degrees F before doing anything else and grease a pizza pan.
2. On a lightly floured surface, roll the bread dough into a large circle about 14-inches across.
3. Place the dough onto the prepared pizza pan and pinch the edges.
4. Cook everything in the oven for about 20-25 minutes.
5. Remove everything from the oven and top with the half of the salad dressing evenly, followed by half of the Swiss cheese, corned beef, remaining salad dressing, sauerkraut and remaining Swiss cheese.
6. Top with the caraway seeds evenly.
7. Cook everything in the oven for about 10 minutes.
8. Remove everything from the oven and top with the chopped pickle.
9. Keep aside for about 5 minutes before slicing.

BACKROAD
Pizza

Prep Time: 15 mins
Total Time: 30 mins

Servings per Recipe: 4
Calories   830 kcal
Fat   46.7 g
Carbohydrates   55.8g
Protein   47.9 g
Cholesterol   139 mg
Sodium   1485 mg

Ingredients

1 lb. ground beef
1 (10.75 oz.) can condensed cream of mushroom soup, undiluted
1 (12 inch) pre-baked thin pizza crust
1 (8 oz.) package shredded Cheddar cheese

Directions

1. Set your oven to 425 degrees F before doing anything else.
2. Heat a large skillet on medium heat and cook the beef till browned completely.
3. Drain the excess grease from the skillet.
4. Place the cream of mushroom soup over the pizza crust evenly and top with the cooked beef, followed by the cheese.
5. Cook everything in the oven for about 15 minutes.

Buttermilk Pizza

Prep Time: 20 mins
Total Time: 1 hr

Servings per Recipe: 8
Calories   624 kcal
Fat   36.4 g
Carbohydrates   45.4g
Protein   28.5 g
Cholesterol   80 mg
Sodium   1962 mg

Ingredients

- 1 lb. ground beef
- 1/4 lb. sliced pepperoni sausage
- 1 (14 oz.) can pizza sauce
- 2 (12 oz.) packages refrigerated buttermilk biscuit dough
- 1/2 onion, sliced and separated into rings
- 1 (10 oz.) can sliced black olives
- 1 (4.5 oz.) can sliced mushrooms
- 1 1/2 C. shredded mozzarella cheese
- 1 C. shredded Cheddar cheese

Directions

1. Set your oven to 400 degrees F before doing anything else and grease a 13x9-inch baking dish.
2. Heat a large skillet on medium-high heat and cook the beef till browned completely.
3. Add the pepperoni and cook till browned and drain the excess grease from the skillet.
4. Stir in the pizza sauce and remove everything from the heat.
5. Cut each biscuit into quarters, and arrange into the prepared baking dish.
6. Place the beef mixture over the biscuits evenly and top them with the onion, olives and mushrooms.
7. Cook everything in the oven for about 20-25 minutes.
8. Now, top everything with the mozzarella and cheddar cheese and cook it all in the oven for about 5-10 minutes.

KID'S FRIENDLY
Pizzas

Prep Time: 25 mins
Total Time: 40 mins

Servings per Recipe: 20
Calories   338 kcal
Fat   21.1 g
Carbohydrates   22.9 g
Protein   13.5 g
Cholesterol   48 mg
Sodium   678 mg

Ingredients

1 lb. ground beef
1 lb. fresh, ground beef sausage
1 onion, chopped
10 oz. processed American cheese, cubed
32 oz. cocktail rye bread

Directions

1. Set your oven to 350 degrees F before doing anything else.
2. Heat a large skillet and cook the sausage and beef till browned completely.
3. Add the onion and cook till tender and drain the excess grease from the skillet.
4. Stir in the processed cheese food and cook till the cheese is melted.
5. On a cookie sheet, place the bread slices and top each slice with a heaping spoonful of the beef mixture.
6. Cook everything in the oven for about 12-15 minutes.

Worcestershire Pizza

Prep Time: 15 mins
Total Time: 30 mins

Servings per Recipe: 8
Calories	349 kcal
Fat	21.7 g
Carbohydrates	20.1 g
Protein	17.5 g
Cholesterol	84 mg
Sodium	1107 mg

Ingredients

- 1/2 lb. lean ground beef
- 1/2 C. diced pepperoni
- 1 1/4 C. pizza sauce
- 1 C. crumbled feta cheese
- 1/2 tsp Worcestershire sauce
- 1/2 tsp hot pepper sauce
- salt and ground black pepper to taste
- cooking spray
- 1 (10 oz.) can refrigerated biscuit dough
- 1 egg yolk
- 1 C. shredded mozzarella cheese

Directions

1. Set your oven to 375 degrees F before doing anything else and grease a cookie sheet.
2. Heat a large skillet on medium-high heat and cook the beef till browned completely.
3. Drain the excess grease from the skillet and reduce the heat to medium.
4. Stir in the pizza sauce, pepperoni, feta, hot pepper sauce, Worcestershire sauce, salt and pepper and stir fry for about 1 minute.
5. Separate the biscuits and arrange onto prepared cookie sheet about 3-inches apart.
6. With the bottom of a glass, press each biscuit to form a 4-inch round biscuit with 1/2-inch rim around the outside edge.
7. In a small bowl, add the egg yolk and 1/4 tsp of the water and beat well.
8. Place about 1/4 C. of the beef mixture in each biscuit cup and top with the mozzarella cheese.
9. Cook everything in the oven for about 15-20 minutes.

BBQ Beef Pizza

🍳 Prep Time: 20 mins
🕐 Total Time: 40 mins

Servings per Recipe: 8
Calories 541 kcal
Fat 22 g
Carbohydrates 62.7g
Protein 26.5 g
Cholesterol 55 mg
Sodium 1384 mg

Ingredients

1 (12 oz.) package Beef Sausage, cut into 1/4-inch slices.
2 (14 oz.) packages 12-inch size Italian pizza crust
2/3 C. prepared barbecue sauce
1 C. thinly sliced red onion
1 green bell pepper, seeded, cut into thin strips
2 C. shredded mozzarella cheese

Directions

1. Set your oven to 425 degrees F before doing anything else.
2. Arrange the pizza crusts onto 2 baking sheets.
3. Spread the barbecue sauce on each crust evenly, followed by the sausage, red onion, pepper and mozzarella cheese.
4. Cook everything in the oven for about 20 minutes.

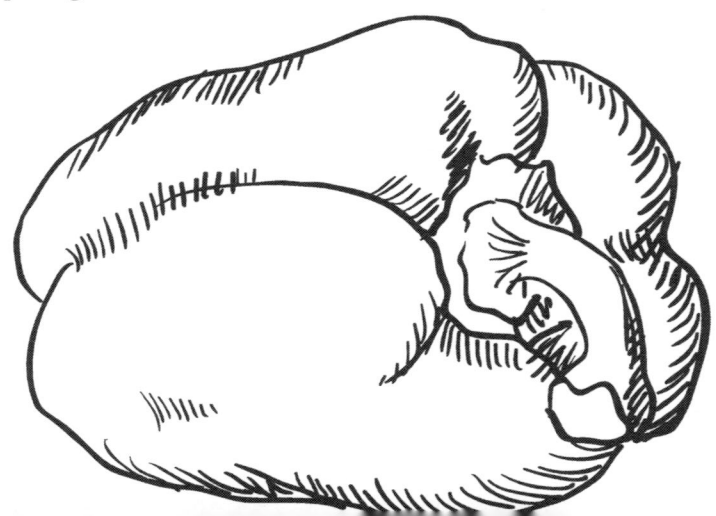

Mexican Style
Pizza

🥣 Prep Time: 45 mins
🕐 Total Time: 1 hr 30 mins

Servings per Recipe: 10
Calories   1376 kcal
Fat   73.5 g
Carbohydrates   1113.3g
Protein   65.6 g
Cholesterol   1197 mg
Sodium   2751 mg

Ingredients

1 lb. ground beef
1 onion, chopped
2 medium tomatoes, chopped
1/2 tsp salt
1/4 tsp pepper
2 tsp chili powder
1 tbsp ground cumin
1 (30 oz.) can refried beans
14 (12 inch) flour tortillas
2 C. sour cream
1 1/4 lb. shredded Colby cheese

1 1/2 lb. shredded Monterey Jack cheese
2 red bell peppers, seeded and thinly sliced
4 green bell peppers, seeded and thinly sliced
1 (7 oz.) can diced green chilies, drained
3 tomatoes, chopped
1 1/2 C. shredded cooked chicken meat
1/4 C. butter, melted
1 (16 oz.) jar picante sauce

Directions

1. Set your oven to 350 degrees F before doing anything else and grease a 15x10-inch jellyroll pan.
2. Heat a large skillet on medium heat and cook the beef till browned completely.
3. Drain the excess grease from the skillet.
4. Add the onion and 2 tomatoes and cook till tender.
5. Stir in the refried beans, chili powder, cumin, salt and pepper and cook until heated completely.
6. Arrange 6 of the tortillas onto the prepared pan with the edges going well over the sides of the pan.
7. Spread the beans mixture over the tortillas evenly, followed by half of the sour cream, 1/3 of the Colby cheese, 1/3 of the Monterey Jack cheese, 1 tbsp of the green chilies, 1/3 of the green pepper

strips, and 1/3 of the red pepper strips and 1/3 of the chopped tomato.

8. Place 4 tortillas over the toppings, and top with the remaining sour cream, followed by the shredded chicken, 1/3 of both cheeses, red and green bell peppers, chilies, and tomatoes.
9. Now, place 4 tortillas, followed by the remaining cheeses, peppers, tomatoes, chilies, and ending with some of the shredded cheese on the top.
10. Fold the overhanging edges inward, and secure with the toothpicks.
11. Brush the tortilla surfaces with the melted butter.
12. Cook everything in the oven for about 35-45 minutes.
13. Remove the toothpicks and keep aside for at least 5 minutes before slicing.
14. Serve with a topping of the picante sauce.

Mediterranean Pizza

Prep Time: 30 mins
Total Time: 40 mins

Servings per Recipe: 8
Calories 519 kcal
Fat 20.4 g
Carbohydrates 56.8g
Protein 30 g
Cholesterol 49 mg
Sodium 1431 mg

Ingredients

- 2 tomatoes, seeded and coarsely chopped
- 1 tsp salt
- 8 oz. shredded mozzarella cheese
- 1 red onion, coarsely chopped
- 1/4 C. chopped fresh basil
- 1/2 tsp ground black pepper
- 2 tbsp olive oil
- 3 fresh jalapeno peppers, chopped
- 1/2 C. sliced black olives
- 1/2 C. sliced fresh mushrooms
- 1/2 C. pizza sauce
- 2 (12 inch) pre-baked pizza crusts
- 8 oz. shredded mozzarella cheese
- 1/4 C. grated Parmesan cheese

Directions

1. Set your oven to 450 degrees F.
2. In a mesh strainer, add the tomatoes and sprinkle with the salt evenly.
3. Keep everything in the sink for about 15 minutes to drain.
4. In a large bowl, mix together the 8 oz. of the mozzarella, drained tomatoes, mushrooms, olives, onion, jalapeño peppers, basil and oil.
5. Place the tomato sauce over the both crusts evenly and top with the tomato mixture, followed by the remaining mozzarella and Parmesan cheese.
6. Cook everything in the oven for about 8-10 minutes.

PIZZA Rigatoni

Prep Time: 20 mins
Total Time: 4 hrs 20 mins

Servings per Recipe: 6
Calories   820 kcal
Fat   43.3 g
Carbohydrates   50.9 g
Protein   53.8 g
Cholesterol   1154 mg
Sodium   2181 mg

Ingredients

- 1 1/2 lb. ground beef
- 1 (8 oz.) package rigatoni pasta
- 1 (16 oz.) package shredded mozzarella cheese
- 1 (10.75 oz.) can condensed cream of tomato soup
- 2 (14 oz.) jars pizza sauce
- 1 (8 oz.) package sliced pepperoni sausage

Directions

1. In a large pan of lightly salted boiling water, cook the pasta for about 8-10 minutes.
2. Drain well and keep aside.
3. Meanwhile, heat a large skillet on medium-high heat and cook the beef till browned completely.
4. Drain the excess grease from the skillet.
5. In a slow cooker place the beef, followed by the pasta, cheese, soup, sauce and pepperoni sausage.
6. Set the slow cooker on Low and cook, covered for about 4 hours.

All Peppers and Onions Pizza

Prep Time: 15 mins
Total Time: 30 mins

Servings per Recipe: 6
Calories	575 kcal
Fat	32.5 g
Carbohydrates	38.9 g
Protein	33 g
Cholesterol	224 mg
Sodium	1028 mg

Ingredients

- 8 oz. ground beef sausage
- 5 eggs, lightly beaten
- 1 (12 inch) prepared pizza crust
- 1 C. ricotta cheese
- 1/4 C. chopped red onion
- 1/4 C. chopped fresh tomato
- 1/4 C. chopped red bell pepper
- 1/4 C. chopped green bell pepper
- 8 oz. shredded mozzarella cheese

Directions

1. Set your oven to 375 degrees F before doing anything else.
2. Heat a large skillet on medium-high heat and cook the sausage till browned completely.
3. Drain the excess grease from the skillet and add the eggs, then cook till eggs are set completely.
4. Arrange the pizza crust on a pizza pan and top with the ricotta cheese, leaving the outer edges.
5. Place the sausage mixture over the ricotta cheese, followed by the onion, tomato, red pepper and green pepper and mozzarella.
6. Cook everything in the oven for about 15 minutes.

I ♥ Pizza

▢ Prep Time: 30 mins
◷ Total Time: 2 hrs 15 mins

Servings per Recipe: 12
Calories   261 kcal
Fat   9.1 g
Carbohydrates   31g
Protein   13.2 g
Cholesterol   18 mg
Sodium   431 mg

Ingredients

3 C. bread flour
1 (.25 oz.) envelope active dry yeast
1 1/4 C. warm water
3 tbsp extra virgin olive oil, divided
3 tbsp chopped fresh rosemary
1 (14 oz.) can pizza sauce
3 C. shredded mozzarella cheese

2 ripe tomatoes, sliced
1 zucchini, sliced
15 slices vegetarian pepperoni
1 (2.25 oz.) can sliced black olives

Directions

1. In a bread machine, add the flour, yeast, water, and 2 tbsp of the olive oil in the order recommended by the manufacturer.
2. Select the Dough setting and press Start.
3. When the cycle is completed, knead rosemary into the dough.
4. Set your oven to 400 degrees F.
5. Divide the dough into three equal sized portions.
6. Shape each dough portion into a heart shape about 1/2-inch thick and coat each portion with the remaining olive oil.
7. Spread a thin layer of pizza sauce over each pizza evenly and top with the cheese, followed by the tomatoes, zucchini, pepperoni, and olives.
8. Cook everything in the oven for about 15-20 minutes.

Vegetarian
Potato Tofu Pizza

Prep Time: 40 mins
Total Time: 50 mins

Servings per Recipe: 2
Calories 916 kcal
Fat 27.4 g
Carbohydrates 123.5g
Protein 53.7 g
Cholesterol 1197 mg
Sodium 1066 mg

Ingredients

- 4 potatoes, shredded
- 1 medium onion, grated
- 2 eggs, beaten
- 1/4 C. all-purpose flour
- 2 tbsp olive oil
- 1 zucchini, thinly sliced
- 1 yellow squash, thinly sliced
- 1 green bell pepper, chopped
- 1 onion, thinly sliced
- 2 cloves garlic, minced
- 6 oz. firm tofu, crumbled
- 2 tomatoes, sliced
- 2 tbsp chopped fresh basil
- 1/2 C. tomato sauce
- 1 C. shredded fat-free mozzarella cheese

Directions

1. Set your oven to 425 degrees F before doing anything else and grease a 12-inch baking dish.
2. In a large bowl, mix together the grated onion, potatoes, flour and egg and place the mixture into the prepared baking dish by pressing gently.
3. Cook everything in the oven for about 15 minutes.
4. Coat the top of the potato crust with the oil and cook everything in the oven for about 10 minutes.
5. Now, place the crust under the broiler and cook for about 3 minutes.
6. Remove the crust from the oven.
7. Again set the oven to 425 degrees F before continuing.
8. In a large bowl, mix together the tofu, green pepper, yellow squash, zucchini, sliced onion and garlic.
9. Heat a large nonstick skillet and sauté the tofu mixture till the vegetables become tender.

10. In a small bowl, mix together the basil and tomato sauce.
11. Place half of the tomato sauce over the crust evenly and top with the cooked vegetables and tomato slices.
12. Spread the remaining sauce on top evenly and sprinkle with the cheese.
13. Cook everything in the oven for about 7 minutes.

Greek Pizza

Prep Time: 20 mins
Total Time: 45 mins

Servings per Recipe:	4
Calories	609 kcal
Fat	26.2 g
Carbohydrates	63.1g
Protein	30 g
Cholesterol	61 mg
Sodium	1531 mg

Ingredients

1 tbsp olive oil
1/2 C. diced onion
2 cloves garlic, minced
1/2 (10 oz.) package frozen chopped spinach, thawed and squeezed dry
1/4 C. chopped fresh basil
2 1/4 tsp lemon juice
1 1/2 tsp dried oregano
ground black pepper to taste
1 (14 oz.) package refrigerated pizza crust
1 tbsp olive oil
1 C. shredded mozzarella cheese
1 large tomato, thinly sliced
1/3 C. seasoned bread crumbs
1 C. shredded mozzarella cheese
3/4 C. crumbled feta cheese

Directions

1. Set your oven to 400 degrees F before doing anything else.
2. In a large skillet, heat 1 tbsp of the oil and sauté the onion and garlic for about 5 minutes. Add the spinach and cook for about 5-7 minutes. Remove everything from the heat and immediately, stir in the oregano, basil, lemon juice and pepper and keep it aside to cool slightly.
3. Unroll the pizza dough on a large baking sheet and coat everything with the remaining 1 tbsp of olive oil.
4. Place the spinach mixture over the dough, leaving a small border at the edges. Place the 1 C. of mozzarella cheese over the spinach.
5. In a bowl, mix together the breadcrumbs and tomato slices till coated completely.
6. Place the tomato slices over the mozzarella cheese, followed by the remaining 1 C. of mozzarella cheese and feta cheese.
7. Cook everything in the oven for about 15 minutes.

PIZZA
Salad

Prep Time: 30 mins
Total Time: 50 mins

Servings per Recipe: 4
Calories   560 kcal
Fat   28.9 g
Carbohydrates   52g
Protein   22.6 g
Cholesterol   41 mg
Sodium   1120 mg

Ingredients

Crust:
1 3/4 C. all-purpose flour
1 envelope Fleischmann's(R) Pizza Crust Yeast
1 1/2 tsp sugar
3/4 tsp salt
2/3 C. very warm water (120 degrees to 130 degrees F)*
3 tbsp extra virgin olive oil
Toppings:
1 tbsp extra virgin olive oil
1/4 tsp Garlic Powder
2 C. shredded mozzarella cheese
1/4 C. chopped onion
1/4 C. chopped or thinly sliced carrots
4 C. chopped romaine lettuce
1 C. chopped fresh tomatoes
1/4 C. prepared Italian salad dressing
1/4 C. shredded Parmesan cheese

Directions

1. Set your oven to 425 degrees F before doing anything else and arrange the rack in the lower third of the oven.
2. Grease a pizza pan.
3. For the crust in a large bowl, add the flour, sugar, yeast, oil and warm water and mix till well combined.
4. Slowly, add the remaining flour and mix till a slightly sticky dough forms.
5. Place the dough on a floured surface and knead it till the dough becomes elastic
6. Place the dough onto the prepared pizza pan and press it.
7. With your fingers, pinch the edges to form the rim.

8. Coat the crust with 1 tbsp of the oil and sprinkle with garlic powder.
9. In a bowl, mix together the carrots, onions and mozzarella cheese.
10. Top the crust with the carrot mixture evenly and cook everything in the oven for about 15-18 minutes.
11. Meanwhile in a bowl, mix together the remaining ingredients.
12. Remove everything from the oven and keep it aside to cool for about 2-3 minutes.
13. Top the pizza with the Parmesan cheese mixture and serve immediately.

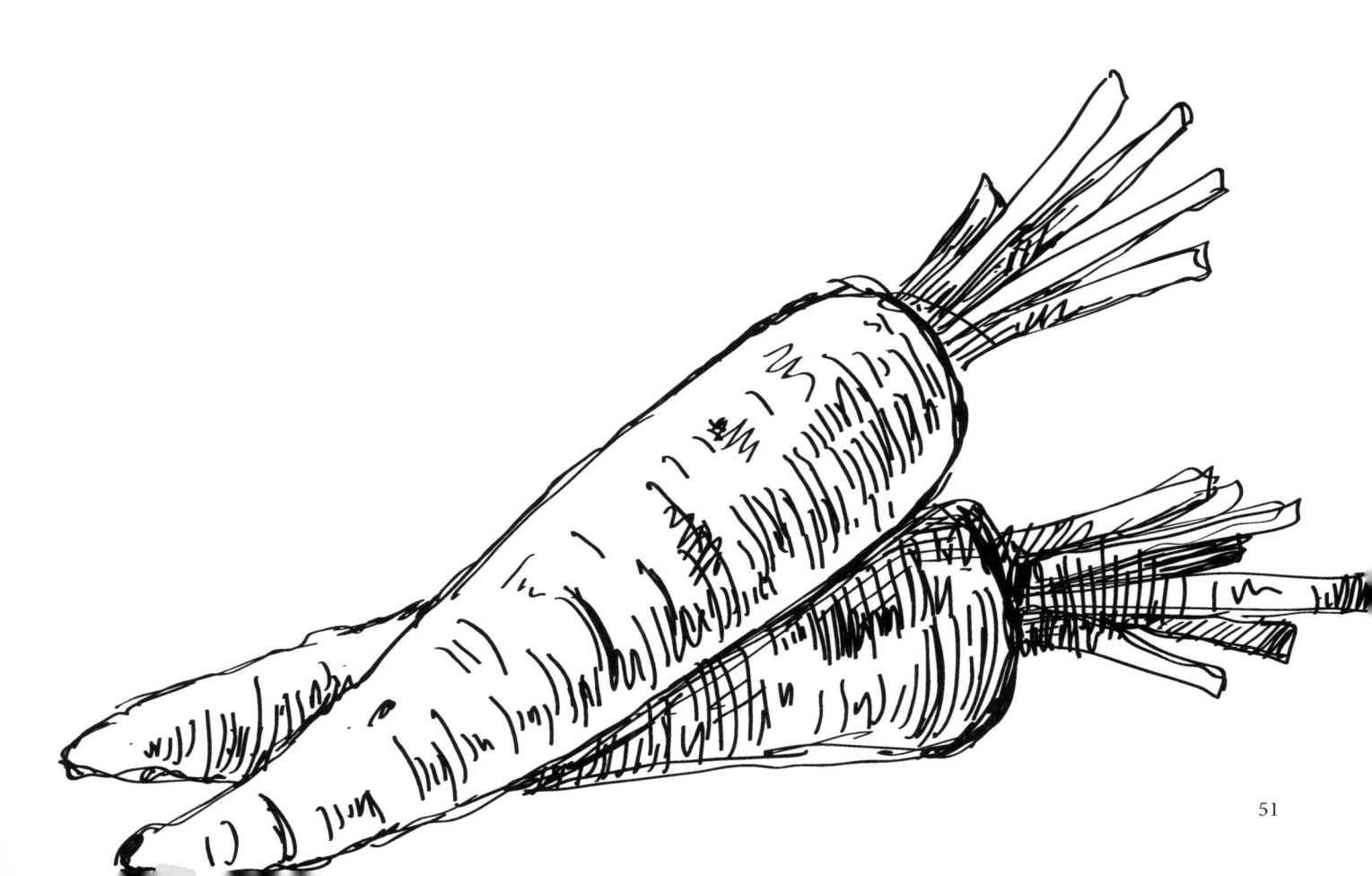

LITTLE TIKE
Dessert Pizza

Prep Time: 30 mins
Total Time: 40 mins

Servings per Recipe: 24
Calories   367 kcal
Fat   20.6 g
Carbohydrates   43.9 g
Protein   5.4 g
Cholesterol   37 mg
Sodium   287 mg

Ingredients

- 1 1/2 C. all-purpose flour
- 2 tsp baking soda
- 1 tsp salt
- 2 1/3 C. rolled oats
- 1 C. butter
- 1 1/2 C. packed brown sugar
- 2 eggs
- 1/2 tsp vanilla extract
- 1 1/2 C. shredded coconut
- 2 C. semisweet chocolate chips
- 1/2 C. chopped walnuts
- 1 C. candy-coated chocolate pieces
- 1 C. peanuts

Directions

1. Set your oven to 350 degrees F before doing anything else and grease 2 (10-inch) pizza pans.
2. In a large bowl, mix together the flour, baking soda and salt.
3. In another bowl, add the butter, eggs, brown sugar and vanilla and beat till smooth.
4. Add the flour mixture into the butter mixture and mix everything until it is all well combined.
5. Fold in the nuts and 1/2 C. of the coconut.
6. Divide the dough into 2 portions and place each portion in the prepared pizza pan, pressing everything into 10-inch circles.
7. Cook everything in the oven for about 10 minutes.
8. Remove everything from the oven and top it all with the remaining coconut, chocolate chips, candies and peanuts.
9. Cook everything in the oven for about 5-10 minutes.

Picnic Mini Pizzas

Prep Time: 30 mins
Total Time: 45 mins

Servings per Recipe: 4
Calories	541 kcal
Fat	28 g
Carbohydrates	45.6 g
Protein	28.3 g
Cholesterol	79 mg
Sodium	1518 mg

Ingredients

- 1/2 lb. ground Italian sausage
- 1/2 tsp garlic salt
- 1/4 tsp dried oregano
- 1 C. crushed pineapple, drained
- 4 English muffins, split
- 1 (6 oz.) can tomato paste
- 1 (8 oz.) package shredded mozzarella cheese

Directions

1. Set your oven to 350 degrees F before doing anything else and lightly, grease a baking sheet.
2. Heat a large skillet on medium-high heat and cook the Italian sausage till browned completely.
3. Drain the excess grease and transfer the sausage into a bowl.
4. Add the pineapple, garlic, oregano and salt and mix well.
5. Place the English muffin halves on the prepared baking sheet in a single layer.
6. Spread tomato sauce over the muffin halves and top with the sausage mixture and mozzarella cheese.
7. Cook everything in the oven for about 10-15 minutes.

TROPICAL
Walnut Pizza

🥣 Prep Time: 5 mins
🕐 Total Time: 45 mins

Servings per Recipe: 6
Calories   442 kcal
Fat   26.5 g
Carbohydrates   48g
Protein   7.8 g
Cholesterol   60 mg
Sodium   567 mg

Ingredients

1 ready-made pizza crust
1 tbsp olive oil
1 (13.5 oz.) container fruit-flavored cream cheese
1 (26 oz.) jar mango slices, drained and chopped
1/2 C. chopped walnuts

Directions

1. Cook the pizza crust in the oven according to package's directions.
2. Coat the crust with the oil evenly.
3. Spread the cream cheese over the crust and top with the chopped mango and nuts.
4. Cut into desired slice and serve.

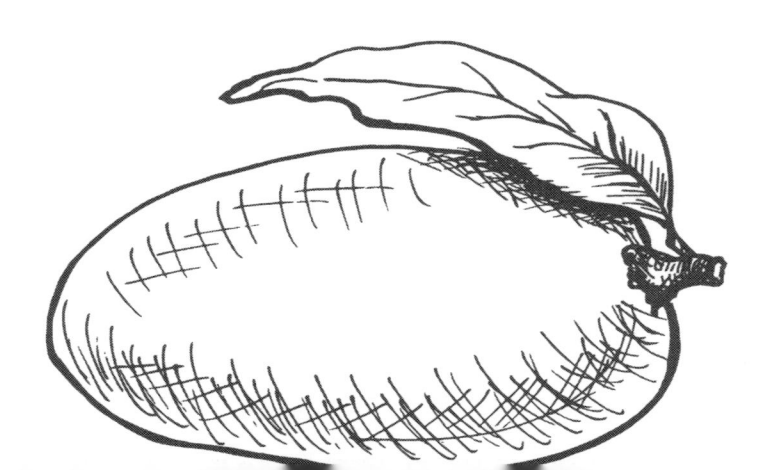

Cranberry Chicken Pizza

Prep Time: 20 mins
Total Time: 40 mins

Servings per Recipe: 4
Calories   865 kcal
Fat   35.4 g
Carbohydrates   91.8g
Protein   47.9 g
Cholesterol   131 mg
Sodium   1262 mg

Ingredients

2 skinless, boneless chicken breast halves, cut into bite-size pieces
1 tbsp vegetable oil
1 (12 inch) prepared pizza crust
1 1/2 C. cranberry sauce
6 oz. Brie cheese, chopped
8 oz. shredded mozzarella cheese

Directions

1. Set your oven to 350 degrees F
2. In a skillet, heat the oil and stir fry the chicken till cooked completely.
3. Spread the cranberry sauce over the prepared pizza crust and top with the chicken, followed by the brie and mozzarella.
4. Cook everything in the oven for about 20 minutes.

SWEET & SALTY
Pizza

🥣 Prep Time: 1 hr
🕐 Total Time: 1 hr 18 mins

Servings per Recipe: 4
Calories   630 kcal
Fat   17.9 g
Carbohydrates   100.8g
Protein   18 g
Cholesterol   22 mg
Sodium   833 mg

Ingredients

1 C. lukewarm water
1 (.25 oz.) envelope active dry yeast
3 C. all-purpose flour
1 tsp vegetable oil
1 tsp salt
8 dried figs
1 medium red onion, thinly sliced
1 tbsp olive oil

1 pinch salt
1 tsp dried thyme
1 tsp fennel seeds
4 oz. goat cheese
1 tbsp olive oil, or as needed

Directions

1. In a large bowl, add the water and sprinkle the yeast on top.
2. Keep everything aside for a few minutes or till it is dissolved completely.
3. Add the flour, salt and oil and mix till a stiff dough forms.
4. Place the dough on a floured surface and knead for about 5 minutes.
5. Transfer the dough into a greased bowl and cover with a kitchen towel.
6. Keep everything aside for about 45 minutes.
7. In a bowl of boiling water, add the figs and keep aside for about 10 minutes.
8. Drain the figs then chop them.
9. Meanwhile in a skillet, heat 1 tbsp of the oil on medium heat and sauté the onions till soft.
10. Reduce the heat to low, and season with the salt.
11. Stir fry for about 5-10 minutes more.

12. Stir in the figs, thyme and fennel seeds and remove everything from the heat.
13. Set your oven to 450 degrees F and lightly grease a pizza pan.
14. Punch down the pizza dough, and spread into a 1/4-inch thick circle.
15. Place the dough onto the prepared pizza pan and brush the surface lightly with the remaining olive oil.
16. Spread the fig mixture over the crust evenly and top everything with the goat cheese in the form of dots.
17. Cook everything in the oven for about 15-18 minutes.

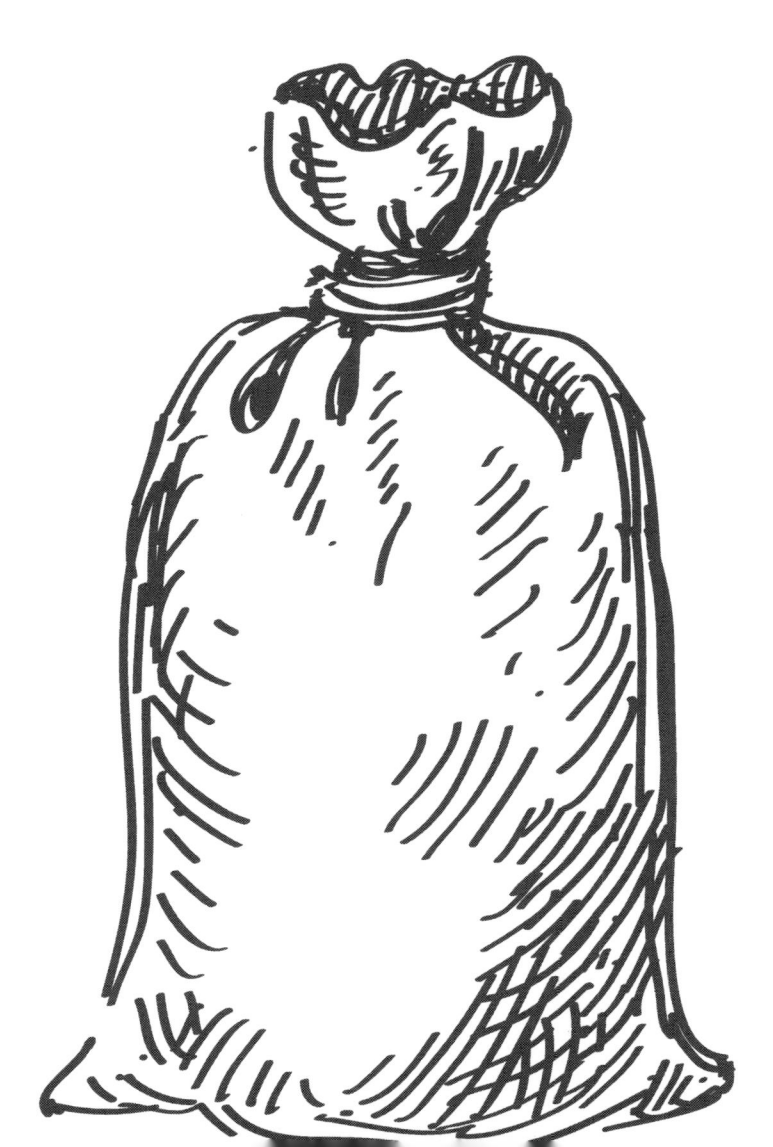

AUTUMNAL
Dijon Pizza

🥣 Prep Time: 20 mins
🕐 Total Time: 35 mins

Servings per Recipe: 6
Calories   427 kcal
Fat   28.4 g
Carbohydrates   34.4g
Protein   11.7 g
Cholesterol   17 mg
Sodium   537 mg

Ingredients

1 pre-baked pizza crust
2 cloves garlic, minced
1 tbsp Dijon mustard
2 sprigs fresh rosemary, chopped
1/4 C. white wine vinegar
1/2 C. olive oil
1/4 C. crumbled blue cheese
salt and pepper to taste
1/4 C. crumbled blue cheese
1/3 C. shredded mozzarella cheese
2 pears - peeled, cored and sliced
1/4 C. toasted walnut pieces

Directions

1. Set your oven to 425 degrees F before doing anything else
2. In a pizza pan, place the pizza crust.
3. Cook everything in the oven for about 5 minutes.
4. Remove everything from the oven and keep it aside to cool completely.
5. In a food processor, add the garlic, rosemary Dijon mustard and vinegar and pulse till combined.
6. While the motor is running, slowly, add the oil and pulse till smooth.
7. Add about 1/4 C. of the blue cheese, salt and pepper and pulse till combined.
8. Spread the vinaigrette over the pizza crust evenly and sprinkle with the remaining blue cheese then mozzarella cheese.
9. Top everything with the pear slices then the toasted walnuts.
10. Cook everything in the oven for about 7-10 minutes.

Mediterranean Pizza II

Prep Time: 20 mins
Total Time: 35 mins

Servings per Recipe: 6
Calories   395 kcal
Fat   16.8 g
Carbohydrates   54.4g
Protein   15.9 g
Cholesterol   23 mg
Sodium   607 mg

Ingredients

- 1 (12 inch) thin prepared pizza crust
- 3 C. chopped bell peppers (red, green, yellow)
- 1 C. sliced red or yellow onion, pulled into rings
- 3 cloves garlic, crushed
- 2 tbsp extra-virgin olive oil
- 1 1/2 tsp dried Italian herbs
- Salt, to taste
- Crushed red pepper flakes, to taste (optional)

Directions

1. Set your oven to 450 degrees F and grease a pizza pan.
2. Place the dough on a pizza pan and press it to the desired thickness.
3. In a bowl, mix together the remaining ingredients except the cheese.
4. Place the mixture over the crust evenly, followed by the cheese
5. Cook everything in the oven for about 10-12 minutes.

GORGONZOLA
Buttery Pizza

Prep Time: 15 mins
Total Time: 55 mins

Servings per Recipe: 12
Calories   241 kcal
Fat   13.7 g
Carbohydrates   17.3g
Protein   10.9 g
Cholesterol   46 mg
Sodium   551 mg

Ingredients

- 1/8 C. butter
- 2 large Vidalia onions, thinly sliced
- 2 tsp sugar
- 1 (10 oz.) package refrigerated pizza dough
- 1 lb. Gorgonzola cheese, crumbled

Directions

1. In a large skillet, melt the butter on medium heat and sauté the onion for about 25 minutes.
2. Stir in the sugar and cook, stirring continuously for about 1-2 minutes.
3. Set your oven to 425 degrees F and grease a pizza pan.
4. Place the dough onto the prepared pizza pan and press it to the desired thickness.
5. Place the onions over the crust evenly, followed by the Gorgonzola.
6. Cook everything in the oven for about 10-12 minutes.

Arugula Grape Pizza

Prep Time: 20 mins
Total Time: 55 mins

Servings per Recipe: 4
Calories	379.2
Fat	13.9g
Carbohydrates	22.4mg
Protein	239.8mg
Cholesterol	59.9g
Sodium	10.9g

Ingredients

- 16 oz. premade pizza dough
- 1/2 C. Pasta Sauce
- 1/2 C. shredded whole milk mozzarella
- 1/2 C. shredded provolone cheese
- 1/4 C. goat cheese, crumbled
- 1/4 C. pine nuts
- 10 red grapes, halved
- 1/4 C. arugula, finely chopped
- 1 tbsp dried rosemary leaves
- 1 tbsp dried oregano
- 1/2 tsp dried cilantro

Directions

1. Set your oven to 475 degrees F before doing anything else and grease a baking sheet.
2. Arrange the pizza dough ball onto the prepared baking sheet and flatten the center of the dough thinly.
3. The crust should be 12-14-inches in diameter.
4. In a bowl, mix together the pasta sauce, arugula, cilantro and oregano.
5. Spread the sauce mixture over the dough evenly.
6. Place the mozzarella and provolone cheeses over the sauce evenly.
7. Top everything with the grapes, followed by the rosemary, goat cheese and pine nuts.
8. Cook everything in the oven for about 11-14 minutes.

FRENCH STYLE
Pizza

🥣 Prep Time: 5 mins
🕐 Total Time: 25 mins

Servings per Recipe: 2
Calories   804.7
Fat   56.6g
Carbohydrates   132.0mg
Protein   1811.7mg
Cholesterol   34.3g
Sodium   41.1g

Ingredients

1 thin pizza crust
2 C. red grapes, sliced in half
1/2 lb. Italian sausage, browned and crumbled
6 oz. fresh goat cheese

extra virgin olive oil
salt and pepper

Directions

1. Set your oven to 450 degrees F before doing anything else.
2. Arrange the pizza crust on a pizza pan.
3. Brush the crust with the oil and sprinkle with the salt and black pepper.
4. Place the sausage over pizza crust, followed by the grapes and goat cheese.
5. Cook everything in the oven for about 13-15 minutes.

French Style Pizza

ENJOY THE RECIPES?

KEEP ON COOKING WITH 6 MORE FREE COOKBOOKS!

Visit our website and simply enter your email address to join the club and receive your 6 cookbooks.

http://booksumo.com/magnet

https://www.instagram.com/booksumopress/

https://www.facebook.com/booksumo/

Printed in Great Britain
by Amazon